Google Pixel Complete & Simplified User manual For Beginners & Seniors

A Complete Step-by-Step User Guide
With Tips & Tricks to Use Your
Phone With Ease

Wesley K. Jackson

Table of Contents

Introduction

The User Guide for the Google Pixel 9a: A Comprehensive Guide to Getting the Most Out of Your Device

We would like to take this opportunity to welcome you to the Google Pixel 9a User Guide, which is your ultimate companion for maximizing the capacity of your smartphone. This guide is intended to assist you in navigating every feature, option, and secret trick that your smartphone has to offer, regardless of whether you are looking to use your Google Pixel for the first time or are an experienced enthusiast.

With its strong performance, beautiful display, and adaptable camera system, the Google Pixel 9a is a smartphone that offers all of these features at a price that is not prohibitive. In order to get the most out of your phone, however, you need to have a solid understanding of its capabilities. With this book, you will get detailed instructions, useful suggestions, and professional guidance on a variety of topics, including: Getting Started: Initialize your device, transfer data, and customize your home screen to suit your preferences.

The Google Pixel 9a's multi-lens configuration is showcased in the book "Mastering the Camera," which provides expert advice on how to take great photographs and movies.

Discover the best practices for fast-charging and energy-saving ways to maximize the life of your cellular device's battery.

Security and privacy may be achieved by establishing fingerprint and face recognition, securing your data, and managing permissions for an application.

Hidden features and shortcuts are a means of unlocking secret tricks that can enhance your user experience and allow you to increase your productivity.

In order to ensure that your phone continues to function without any interruptions, it is essential to undertake troubleshooting and maintenance tasks.

This tutorial will guarantee that you become a Google Pixel 9a in no time at all by providing you with easily understandable explanations, handy screenshots, and directions that are simple to follow.

Prepared to discover everything that your phone is capable of? It's time to get started!

Your adventure with the Google Pixel 9a starts right now.

Chapter 1: Overview of Your Google Pixel 9A

Google created the Pixel 9a, a smartphone that blends robust features, seamless operation, and simple access to Google services. The Pixel 9a is simple to use and provides a clean Android experience, regardless of whether you're migrating from another brand or using smartphones for the first time. This phone is well-known for its excellent camera, quick software upgrades, and compatibility with Google services and apps.

Important attributes and details

Here is a brief overview of the features that set the Pixel 9a apart:

• Display: An excellent screen that's ideal for playing games, watching videos, and surfing the web.

• Camera: The Pixel 9a carries on the legacy of Pixel phones' renownedly good cameras. It has strong features like Portrait Mode (for selfies that seem professional), Night Sight (for amazing pictures in low light), and more.

• Battery Life: You won't have to worry about continuously charging the Pixel 9a thanks to its all-day battery life.

• Performance: You can run programs, play games, and switch between tasks without any lag when your processor is quick.

• Google Assistant: With just your voice, this personal assistant can assist you with tasks, manage smart home appliances, send messages, and much more.

• Security: To protect your phone and data, the Pixel 9a has a fingerprint sensor in addition to other security features like facial recognition.

• Software: Since it's a Google device, Google updates it directly, so you'll always have the most recent Android version with the newest security patches and features.

• Storage: Sufficient space to store your apps, pictures, movies, and other data. If you need extra space, you can save files online thanks to its integration with Google services like Google Drive.

What's inside the box?

When you open the Google Pixel 9a's box, you'll discover the following:

1.The primary phone is the Google Pixel 9a.

2.The USB-C cable is used to connect to other devices and charge the phone.

3.A plug used to charge the Pixel 9a is called a power adapter.

4.A tiny instrument for opening the SIM card tray is called a SIM Ejector Tool.

5.Quick Start Guide: An easy-to-follow manual to get you started with your phone.

6.Information on the warranty on your phone, in case you require repairs or assistance.

Note: It's possible that the Google Pixel 9a will not include microSD cards or headphones. If you desire some of them, you may need to purchase them separately.

How to Begin Using Your Pixel 9a

Here's how to begin using your Google Pixel 9a now that you know what's inside the box:

1.**Put the SIM card in**:

o Insert your SIM card after opening the SIM card tray with the SIM ejector tool. Your phone joins the mobile network in this manner.

2.**Turn on your phone**:

o Hold down the phone's side power button until the Google logo shows up on the screen.

The welcome screen will appear as your phone boots up.

3.**Configure Your Phone**:

o Choose your language: Decide which language you would like your gadget to speak.

o Connect to Wi-Fi: To access the internet and download updates and apps, connect to a Wi-Fi network.

o Log in to your Google Account: To sync your contacts, apps, and images, log in right away if you already have a Google account (such as Gmail or YouTube).

o Configure a screen lock: You will be prompted to create a pattern, password, or PIN for extra protection. Later on, you can also enable facial unlock or fingerprint recognition.

4.Complete the setup:

o Your phone will walk you through a few more stages, such as transferring data from an old phone, configuring Google Assistant, and customizing your settings, after you've signed in and set up security.

After completing these steps, your Google Pixel 9a is ready for use! You can begin by snapping your first picture using the camera, downloading apps from the Google Play Store, or browsing your home screen.

That concludes Chapter 1! You are now prepared to use your Google Pixel 9a since you have a fundamental understanding of it. We'll go into greater detail about your new device's features and capabilities in the upcoming chapters.

Chapter 2: Configuring Your Pixel 9a

Well done on your new Google Pixel 9a purchase! Let's now walk you through the process of getting your gadget operational. We'll go over everything in this chapter, including how to set up Google services, move data from your old device, and insert your SIM card.

Putting the microSD and SIM card in (if applicable)

You must enter a SIM card into your Google Pixel 9a before you can use it. Your phone can utilize data, make calls, and connect to the mobile network thanks to the SIM card. A microSD card, which provides additional capacity for pictures, movies, and apps, is also supported by some phones. Here's how to accomplish it:

Putting the SIM card in:

1.Locate the SIM tray: The SIM card tray is located next to a little hole on the side of the Pixel 9a.

2.Utilise the SIM ejector tool: Carefully place the SIM ejector tool—which comes in the box—into the hole. The SIM tray will pop out of the phone as a result.

3.Put your SIM card into the tray to insert it. Make sure the card fits tightly by aligning it correctly.

4.Reinstalling the tray requires gently pushing it back into the phone until it is securely in place.

Note: To increase the amount of storage on your Pixel 9a, you may also put a microSD card in the same tray if it has one. Verify that it is put in the proper direction.

Turning Your Pixel 9a On

Let's turn on your Pixel 9a now that your SIM card is in position.

1.Locate the power button on the side of your phone, then press and hold it for a select few seconds.

2.Await the Google logo: The phone is starting up when the Google logo appears on the screen after a few seconds.

Tip: Verify that the battery is charged if your phone isn't turning on. If not, try turning it on again after plugging it in using the charging cable and adapter that come with it.

First Setup Instructions

Your Pixel 9a will walk you through a few initial setup tasks when it initially turns on. This is what to anticipate:

1. **Choose your language**:

• Choosing the language you wish to use on your device will be the first task you are required to do. There are many different languages available, so pick the one you feel most at ease speaking.

2. **Establish a Wi-Fi connection:**

• After choosing your language, you must establish a Wi-Fi connection. You can use this to download programs, updates, and anything else you'll need for setup.

o Enter your Wi-Fi password and select your network from the list.

o You can skip this step if you don't have Wi-Fi, but downloading apps and updates will require Wi-Fi later.

3. Access your Google account by logging in:

• After that, a popup to log into your Google account will appear. This is where you'll log in if you have a Gmail account or any other Google services (like YouTube, Google Photos, etc.).

To sign in, enter your email address and password if you already have a Google account.

o During this process, you can create a Google account if you don't already have one. To make a new account, just follow the directions.

Why is it crucial to log into your Google account?

• You can use Google services like Gmail, Google Play Store, Google Photos, and more by logging in.

• It also aids in backing up your data, including contacts, images, and app settings, so you can quickly recover it in the event that you need to replace your phone or reset it.

Data Transfer from Your Previous Device

You should move your contacts, texts, apps, and other crucial data to your new Pixel 9a if you're upgrading from another phone. Thankfully, Google's "Switch to Android" option makes this simple. Here's how to accomplish it:

Option 1: **For a quicker transfer, use a cable**.

1. Link both phones: Link your previous phone to the Pixel 9a using a USB-C to USB-C connection (or the provided adaptor if your old phone uses a different socket).

2. **Observe the instructions**: Your Pixel 9a will ask you what you wish to move (contacts, apps, messages, pictures, etc.) as it walks you through the procedure.

3. **Finish the transfer**: Your data will be accessible on your new Pixel 9a after the transfer is complete.

Option 2: **Without a cable, use Google Backup**

1. Make sure your old phone's data is backed up to Google Drive, the company's cloud

service. Your contacts, apps, and pictures will all be automatically backed up on the majority of Android phones.

2.**Restore on your Pixel 9a**: The Pixel 9a will offer to restore your data from the cloud backup when you check in to your Google account during the setup process. Your old data will be moved to your new device if you simply follow the directions.

Tip: If you have been backing up your photos and videos on your old smartphone, you can also use the Google Photos app to move them.

Configuring Google Services

You'll be asked to configure a few Google services on your Pixel 9a after finishing the basic setup and moving your data. Your phone will become more safe and useful with these services.

1. **Google Assistant**:

• Google Assistant is a voice-activated artificial intelligence tool that assists you with a variety of tasks, like sending messages, scheduling reminders, and checking the weather.

• Pressing and holding the home button or saying "Hey Google" will activate it.

• To configure Google Assistant on your Pixel 9a, adhere to the on-screen directions. In order for it to understand your commands, you may be requested to teach it your voice.

2. **Google Pay**:

• You must set up Google Pay if you wish to use your Pixel 9a for contactless payments. With simply a tap of your phone, you may pay at establishments that accept NFC payments after linking your credit or debit cards to the Google Pay app.

• To configure your payment methods, launch the Google Pay app from the Google Play Store and adhere to the setup directions.

3. **Google Cloud Backup**:

• Google provides cloud backup for your contacts, data, and apps. Turn on Google's backup tool to make sure your data is always backed up and available. This allows you to recover everything from the cloud in the event that you misplace or reset your phone.

• Verify that Google Backup is enabled by going to Settings > System > Backup.

That concludes Chapter 2! The setup of your Google Pixel 9a is now complete. You've set up important Google services, moved your data, logged into your Google account, and connected to Wi-Fi. We'll go over how to get the most of your phone in the upcoming chapters, including how to use apps, adjust settings, and maintain security.

Chapter Three: Getting Around the Google Pixel 9a

Let's start using your phone now that your Google Pixel 9a is configured. This chapter will go over how to customize your home screen, manage widgets and notifications, comprehend the status bar, use gestures for navigation, and interact with the home screen. You will be able to use your phone with ease and customize it to your liking by the conclusion of this chapter.

Comprehending the Home Screen's Design

All of your apps, settings, and features are accessible from the Home Screen, which is the primary screen of your Google Pixel 9a. What can be found on the home screen is broken down as follows:

Important Components:

1.**App Icons**: These are the symbols for the programs you use most frequently, such as Camera, Messages, and Phone. To arrange your home screen, you can add or remove these.

2.**Search Bar**: You can easily search the web or locate programs, contacts, or settings with the search bar located at the top of the screen.

3.**Dock**: Your favorite programs, such as Chrome, Messages, and Phone, can be placed in the "dock" at the bottom of your screen. Regardless of the screen you're on, these applications will always be simple to use.

4.**Home Screen Pages**: Your home screen is composed of multiple pages rather than a single page. In addition to having numerous home screens for various app organizations, you can swipe left or right to view more pages.

5.**App Drawer**: All of your installed apps are kept in this folder. Swipe up from the bottom of the screen to get to it. It functions similarly to a storage area for all of your apps, not just those that are visible on your home screen.

Getting Around With Gestures

For simpler navigation, the Pixel 9a employs gesture navigation rather than physical buttons. Here's how to navigate your phone with gestures:

Fundamental Motions:

1.Navigate to the Home Screen:

o From the bottom of the screen, swipe up. No matter where you are on the phone, this returns you to your home screen.

2.Change Apps:

o Hold while you swipe up. This will enable you to quickly move between the apps you've recently used. Any app can be opened by tapping on it, and it can be closed by swiping up.

3.Return to the Home Screen:

o You can swipe from the screen's left or right edge. This will return you to the previous page or screen.

4. Launch Google Assistant:

From the bottom corner, swipe. With this motion, you can launch Google Assistant and use voice commands like "Play music" or "Set a timer."

Tip: You can adjust your settings if you would rather use the conventional navigation buttons (Back, Home, and Recent). Go to System > Gestures > Settings, then choose "3-button navigation."

Using Quick Settings and the Status Bar

Two essential components for controlling your phone's settings and notifications are the Status Bar and Quick Settings.

The status bar

The Status Bar is located at the top of your screen. This bar displays crucial details about your device, including:

• **Wi-Fi Signal**: Indicates whether you are linked to Wi-Fi and how strong the signal is.

• **Battery Icon**: Shows the level of your battery right now.

• **Mobile Signal**: Shows the strength of the signal and whether your phone is linked to a mobile network.

• **Time**: Displays the time right now.

• Notifications: Warnings about upgrades to apps, emails, or texts. An icon in the status bar indicates that a notice is awaiting you.

Quick Settings:

Swipe down from the top of your screen to reach Quick Settings. A panel with toggles for several settings will then appear, such as:

• **WiFi**: Activate or deactivate your WiFi.

• **Bluetoot**h: Easily pair with Bluetooth-enabled devices, such as speakers or headphones.

• **Do Not Disturb**: To prevent disruptions, temporarily disable notifications.

• Brightness: Modify the brightness of your screen.

• **Aero plane Mode**: Turn off Bluetooth, Wi-Fi, and the mobile network when you need to conserve battery life or while in flight.

Any of these icons can be tapped to activate or deactivate functions. Additional settings like Location, Mobile Hotspot, and Battery Saver will appear if you slide down once more.

Tip: Tap the pencil icon in the lower left corner to change Quick Settings. This lets you reorganize icons to make them more accessible.

Personalizing Your Home Screen

Now that you understand how to use your Pixel 9a, let's customize your home screen so that it is genuinely unique to you. You can add shortcuts for easy access, rearrange apps, and modify items like your wallpaper.

1. **Modify Your Background**:

To modify your home screen's background image, or wallpaper:

1.Any blank area on the home screen can be long-pressed.

2.Select "Wallpaper & Style."

3.You have the option to upload your own image or select from a variety of wallpaper categories, such as static and live wallpapers.

4.After choosing your favorite wallpaper, click Set Wallpaper.

2. **Transfer or Delete Apps**:

You can rearrange your home screen by moving or deleting apps in the manner described below:

1.To move an app, tap and hold the icon of the app. On the home screen, drag it to a new location.

2.Tap and hold the app icon to remove it. Drag it to the "Remove" section at the top of the screen if you wish to keep it on the device but remove it from the home screen. Drag it to Uninstall if you wish to remove it.

3. **Make folders**:

To put related programs (Apps) together, you can make folders. To make a folder:

1.Hold down a tap on an app icon.

2.To group it with another app, drag it over it. It will automatically create a folder.

3.You can drag more apps into the folder and give it a name.

4. **Include Widgets**:

With widgets, you can view app information on your home screen without ever having to open the app. To add one, follow these steps:

1.On your home screen, long press on an empty area.

2.Press the Widgets button.

3.Select the widget you wish to add by tapping on it after looking through the others.

4.Choose the widget's size and where you want it to show up on your home screen.

The weather, calendar, music player, Google Assistant, and news updates are a few examples of practical widgets.

Handling Widgets and Notifications

While widgets allow you to quickly access crucial data or activities, notifications let you keep informed about vital information.

Handling Notifications:

Notifications show up in the Status Bar at the top of your screen when they arrive. This is how to deal with them:

1.**View notifications**: To view your alerts, swipe down from the top of your screen to bring up the notification shade.

2.**Clear notifications**: Swipe a notification to the side to get rid of it. Tap Clear All to get rid of all notifications.

3.**Manage notifications**: Go to Settings > Apps & Notifications > Notifications to manage how apps alert you. From here, you may alter the how each app's notifications look, for as by disabling sound or vibration.

Tip: You can dismiss a notice by swiping it to the left or right. It opens the relevant app when you tap on it.

That concludes Chapter 3! You now know how to use gestures, access the status bar and quick settings, browse the Google Pixel 9a, comprehend the layout of the home screen, and personalize your home screen. You are now prepared to begin making the most of your phone! We'll look at setting up Bluetooth and other connections, managing mobile networks, and connecting to Wi-Fi in the upcoming chapter.

Chapter 4: Establishing Mobile Network and Wi-Fi Connections

We will go over every method in this chapter for connecting your Google Pixel 9a to the internet and other networks, including Bluetooth, Wi-Fi, mobile data, and VPNs. Additionally, you will learn how to control these connections' parameters and utilize Aero plane mode as necessary.

Making a Wi-Fi Network Connection

One of the most popular methods for accessing the internet is Wi-Fi, which is usually quicker and more dependable than mobile data. To connect your Pixel 9a to a Wi-Fi network, follow these steps:

How to Establish a Wi-Fi Connection:

1.Launch Quick Settings:

o To access the Quick Settings panel, swipe down from the top of the screen.

2.Activate Wi-Fi:

o To activate Wi-Fi, tap the symbol if it's not on. When activated, the icon will change to either blue or white.

3.Select a Network:

o Your phone will automatically search for available networks after you turn on Wi-Fi. To connect to a Wi-Fi network, tap on it.

4.Put in the password:

o You will be asked to enter the Wi-Fi password if the network is secured. After entering it, select Connect.

5. Verify the Connection:

o To verify that you are online, the Wi-Fi symbol in the status bar will display the signal strength after you have connected.

Advice: Your phone will automatically rejoin to the same Wi-Fi networks when they are within range if you frequently connect to them (at home, at work, etc.).

Controlling Wi-Fi Configurations

Managing saved networks, customizing advanced settings, and making sure your phone connects safely are just a few of the options available on your Pixel 9a for managing your Wi-Fi connections.

Advanced Configuration for Wi-Fi:

1.Go to the Wi-Fi Settings:

o Select Wi-Fi under Settings > Network & Internet. This will display every network that is available.

2.Conserve Networks:

o Your phone will automatically remember the connection for later use when you connect to a network. In the Wi-Fi settings, you may see saved networks under Saved networks.

3.Wi-Fi Settings Toggle:

o Wi-Fi options allow you to change things like:

When stronger Wi-Fi becomes available, the Wi-Fi assistant lets you switch to it immediately.

Maintain Wi-Fi connectivity while you sleep, which enables your phone to remain connected to the network even when it is not in use.

4.Ignore a Network:

o Tap the network name and choose Forget to delete a saved Wi-Fi network. By doing this, you can prevent your Pixel from automatically connecting to that network.

5.Make use of Wi-Fi calling:

o You can activate Wi-Fi calling to make and receive calls via Wi-Fi if you live in an area with strong Wi-Fi but poor cell reception. If Wi-Fi calling is available, turn it on by going to Settings > Network & Internet > Wi-Fi calling.

Configuring Mobile Data and Navigation

When you're not using Wi-Fi, you can still access the internet on your phone using mobile data. When you're travelling outside of your carrier's coverage region, roaming allows you to utilize mobile data.

Turn on mobile data:

1.Activate mobile data:

o Swipe down from the top of the screen to access Quick Settings.

o To activate Mobile Data, tap its symbol. When mobile data is enabled, the icon will change to either blue or white.

2.Verify Data Usage:

o Select Settings > Network & Internet > Mobile network > Data use to keep an eye on your data usage. To prevent overages, you can establish data consumption restrictions or warnings here.

Configuring Roaming:

1.Activate roaming:

o You must enable roaming in order to utilise mobile data when you are outside of your carrier's coverage area.

To enable roaming services, navigate to Settings > Network & Internet > Mobile network > Roaming and enable data roaming.

Important: It's a good idea to enquire about roaming fees with your carrier because roaming may result in additional charges.

Making Use of Aeroplane Mode

Your phone's Aeroplane Mode feature instantly disables all wireless connections, including Bluetooth, Wi-Fi, and mobile data. It's helpful when you need to save battery life, when you're flying, or in specific public areas.

Activating Aeroplane Mode:

1.Quick Settings:

o To access Quick Settings, swipe down from the top of your screen.

o To activate Aeroplane Mode, tap its icon. Upon activation, all wireless connections—

including Bluetooth, mobile data, and Wi-Fi—will be turned off.

2.**Disabling Aeroplane Mode**:

o To return to the internet, just tap the Quick Settings button for Aeroplane Mode once more.

Tip: By pressing the appropriate icons in Quick Settings, you may manually turn on Bluetooth and Wi-Fi while Aeroplane Mode is selected. In this manner, you can continue to use Bluetooth or Wi-Fi while turning off mobile data.

Linking Up with Bluetooth Devices

Bluetooth enables wireless connections between your phone and a variety of gadgets, including speakers, headphones, and automobile systems. Here's how to configure it:

Setting up a Bluetooth connection:

1.Activate Bluetooth:

o To access Quick Settings, swipe down from the top of the screen.

o To activate Bluetooth, tap the symbol.

2.Setting Up a Bluetooth Device Pairing:

o Your Pixel 9a will search for compatible devices as soon as Bluetooth is enabled.

To pair a new device, navigate to Settings > Connected devices.

o A list of available devices will appear on your phone. To connect a device, such as a speaker or headphones, tap on its name.

3.If required, enter the pairing code:

o A pairing code might be requested by certain Bluetooth devices. Tap Pair after following the directions on the device's screen.

4.Unpairing or disconnecting:

o To disconnect a device, select Disconnect after tapping on the device name in Settings > Connected devices.

To fully unpair a device, choose Forget.

Configuring a Virtual Private Network

When utilising public Wi-Fi networks, a virtual private network, or VPN, is a secure connection that helps safeguard your privacy.

Configuring a Virtual Private Network:

1.Go to the VPN settings:

o Select Network & Internet > VPN under Settings.

2.Install a VPN:

o Select Add VPN and input the required data (such as the login, password, and VPN provider details). These details are available from your VPN provider, which could be a third-party business or your employer.

3.Establish a VPN connection:

o To connect, tap on the VPN name after it has been configured. If necessary, your phone will ask for your username and password.

4.Unplug from the VPN:

o Return to Settings > Network & Internet > VPN, then select Disconnect to disconnect.

Use a VPN only when absolutely required, especially if your connection is poor. VPN connections can cause your internet speed to decrease.

That concludes Chapter 4! You now understand how to use Aeroplane mode, pair your Pixel 9a with Bluetooth devices, control mobile data, set up roaming, connect to Wi-Fi, and establish a VPN connection. We'll explore how to take amazing pictures and films with the Pixel 9a's camera in the upcoming chapter!

Chapter 5: Sending Messages and Making Calls

We'll go over how to send and receive text messages, use Google Assistant for hands-free calling, handle voicemail, and make and receive calls in this chapter. Let's begin with the fundamentals of using your Google Pixel 9a for communication.

Voice Call Making and Receiving

On the Google Pixel 9a, making and receiving calls is easy and straightforward. Here's how to call someone:

Putting in a Call:

1.To launch the Phone app, tap on its icon from your app drawer or home screen. It resembles a green phone receiver.

2.Enter the number:

o To find someone in your contacts list, press the Contacts tab or manually dial a number using the Keypad.

3.Tap the Call Button: To initiate a call, tap the Call icon, which is a green phone receiver, after inputting the number or choosing the contact.

Getting a Call:

• The incoming number or contact name will show up on your screen as a call comes in.

• You can tap the Answer button or swipe up to answer the call.

• You can hit the Decline button or swipe down to reject a call.

Additionally, you can use the Speakerphone, Mute, or Hold choices that appear on the screen when the call is active.

Organizing Favorites and Contacts

You keep the phone numbers, email addresses, and other contact information of the people you frequently interact with in your contacts. Here's how to deal with them:

How to Add a New Contact:

1.Launch the Contacts application.

2.Either create a new contact or tap the plus (+) symbol.

3.Input the individual's name, contact information (phone and email), and any other pertinent information.

4.When you're finished, press Save.

Noting Favourites:

To add a contact to your favourites list:

1.Launch the Contacts application.

2.Locate the contact you wish to add to your favourites.

3.Next to their name, tap the star icon. They are now a favourite if they have a solid star.

Selecting the Favourites tab in the Phone app allows you to instantly call or message your favourites.

Using Hands-Free Calling with Google Assistant

Making calls without touching your phone is simple with Google Assistant. To utilize it for hands-free calling, follow these steps:

1.Turn on Google Assistant:

To activate Google Assistant, either press and hold the Home button or say "Hey Google."

2.Place the Call:

To get Google Assistant to listen, just say "Dial [phone number]" or "Call [contact name]".

3.The Call Will Be Made by Google Assistant:

o Google Assistant will call the number or contact you specified automatically.

Tip: While you're working, you can also ask Google Assistant to check your missed calls or send a text.

Text Message Transmission with SMS, MMS, and RCS

Text messages can be sent with the Google Pixel 9a in a number of forms, including RCS (Rich Communication Services), MMS (Multimedia Messaging Service), and SMS (Short Message Service).

How to send an MMS or SMS:

1.Launch the app called Messages.

2.To start a new message, tap the plus (+) symbol or select Start Chat.

3.Either select a contact from your list or enter the recipient's phone number.

4.Use the text field to type your message.

5.To transmit a picture or video (MMS), tap the paperclip-shaped attachment button, choose the desired media, and then press transmit.

What Makes RCS, MMS, and SMS Different?

• SMS: Typical text messages, which only contain text and little attachments like images.

• Multimedia messages, or MMSs, let you send voice, video, and picture files.

• RCS: Rich Communication Services, which is compatible with your Pixel 9a and many other Android smartphones, is an enhanced messaging system with additional features like read receipts and typing indicators.

Note: You and the recipient of the message must have devices and carriers that support RCS in order to utilize it.

Using Chat Features in Google Messages

Your Pixel 9a's default messaging app is Google Messages, which offers richer messaging experiences with chat capabilities like RCS. To activate and utilize chat functionalities, follow these steps:

1.Turn on RCS:

o Launch the Messages application.

o Press the menu icon (three dots) in the upper-right corner.

o Select Chat Features under Settings.

o Turn on the chat functions. With features like typing indicators, read receipts, and high-quality media, you can send and receive messages via Wi-Fi or mobile data.

2.Chat using RCS Now:

o You will see indicators such as "Typing..." or "Read by [contact name]" when you send a message to someone who has RCS activated as well.

o You don't have to worry about SMS/MMS limits while sending larger photos, videos, and other media assets.

Configuring Voicemail

When you miss a call, voicemail allows you to hear voice messages. To configure it on your Google Pixel 9a, follow these steps:

1.Launch the Phone application.

2.In the upper-right corner, tap the three dots.

3.Select Voicemail under Settings.

4.To configure your voicemail, adhere to the guidelines. Typically, this entails creating a voicemail password and recording a greeting.

Voicemail Access:

• Tap the Voicemail tab in the Phone app to view your voicemail.

• Voicemail messages can be listened to, deleted, or saved from this interface.

Advice: Some carriers let you reach voicemail by pressing the dial pad's 1 key.

Chapter 6: Utilizing the Camera

We'll examine the Google Pixel 9a's potent photography features in this chapter. The Pixel 9a's camera provides everything you need to produce stunning pictures, whether you're taking pictures, making videos, or editing your own photos.

An Overview of the Camera Features of the Pixel 9a

The camera on the Pixel 9a has many strong capabilities, such as the capacity to shoot beautiful pictures in various lighting scenarios, take portraits, and more. Among the salient characteristics are:

• Night Sight: Enables you to capture crisp images in dimly lit areas.

• Portrait Mode: Gives your subject a polished, blurred background (bokeh effect).

• Wide-Angle Lens: Excellent for group or landscape photography, it captures more of the scene.

Using the Front and Rear Cameras to Take Pictures

To use the rear camera to snap a picture:

1.Launch the Camera app, which is typically located on your home screen.

2.Take a picture of your subject.

3.To snap a picture, tap the shutter button, which is represented by the circle icon.

For selfies, to switch to the front-facing camera:

1.In the Camera app, tap the camera switch icon, which resembles a round arrow.

2.You may take selfies just like you would with the rear camera once the front camera is turned on.

Making Use of Portrait Mode, Night Sight, and Other Unique Camera Settings

Night Vision:

Even in extremely low light, Night Sight enables you to snap brilliant, crisp pictures. When you're in an area with little light:

1.Launch the Camera application.

2.To enter Night Sight mode, swipe left.

3.Hold steady for a few seconds while aiming the camera at your subject. To get the greatest shot, the camera will automatically adjust.

Mode of Portrait:

To capture a hazy background in a portrait:

1.Launch the Camera application.

2.To enter portrait mode, swipe.

3.The bokeh effect is automatically applied by the camera when you frame your subject, producing a portrait that looks professional.

Additional Camera Modes:

• Panoramic: Excellent for expansive landscape photographs. Take a wide picture by swiping to the Panorama mode.

• Video: Press the record button after swiping to the Video mode to start recording.

Taking Videos

To capture videos:

1.Launch the Camera application.

2.To access Video mode, swipe.

3.To begin recording, hit the record button; to stop, tap it once again.

Retouching and Distributing Images and Videos

You may modify images or movies directly from the Photos app after taking them:

1.Launch the Photos application.

2.To edit a picture or video, tap on it.

3.Press the Edit icon, which resembles a pencil.

4.Filters, contrast, and brightness can all be changed.

After you're satisfied with your changes, click Share to share your image or video on social media, by email, or by text.

Organizing and Creating Backups with Google Photos

To make sure you never lose your images or videos, Google Photos automatically backs them up to the cloud. Additionally, you can search and arrange your photos by date, location, or even by the subjects.

1.Launch the Google Photos application.

2.To access settings, tap the three dots in the upper-right corner.

3.To have your photos uploaded to Google Drive automatically, turn on Backup & Sync.

That brings Chapters 5 and 6 to a close! You now understand how to use your Google

Pixel 9a to take stunning pictures, send messages, make calls, and use Google Assistant for hands-free communication. We'll then go into how to use Google Assistant to manage daily tasks and operate your phone.

Using Google Assistant in Chapter 7

Google Assistant is a voice-activated virtual assistant driven by artificial intelligence. It can navigate, play music, send texts, make calls, set reminders, and much more. Now let's explore how to configure and utilize Google Assistant on your Pixel 9a.

Google Assistant: What is it?

Google's AI technology powers Google Assistant, a smart assistant. It saves you time and provides a hands-free experience by assisting you in doing tasks on your device with voice commands. Google Assistant is capable of:

• Make calls and send texts

Play videos and music.

• Obtain news, sports, and weather information.

• Manage smart gadgets (should you have any linked smart home appliances)

• Locate and obtain directions

• Configure timers, alerts, and reminders.

Turning on and personalizing Google Assistant

Your Pixel 9a comes with Google Assistant pre-installed, and activating it is simple. To begin, follow these steps:

Turning on Google Assistant:

1.Activating Voice:

Just say "Hey Google" or "Ok Google" to make the Assistant active.

2.Activating a Button:

o To enable Google Assistant on your Pixel 9a, press and hold the Home button.

Tip: If "Google Assistant" isn't responding, make sure it's enabled in your settings. Verify that Google Assistant is activated by going to Settings > Google > Search, Assistant & Voice > Google Assistant.

Personalizing Google Assistant:

1.Personalize Google Assistant:

o Go to Settings > Google > Search, Assistant & Voice > Google Assistant.

o Here, you may modify settings including the Assistant's voice, language, and personalized recommendations.

2.Voice Match:

o Google Assistant utilizes speech Match to detect your speech and offer personalized responses. Under the Google Assistant settings, tap Voice Match to train it to recognize your voice.

3.Linking Accounts:

o You can integrate your Google account, smart home gadgets, and other services (like Spotify or YouTube) to make your Assistant smarter.

Using Voice Commands to Control Your Device

Once Google Assistant is set up, you can use voice commands to control many functions on your phone. Here are a few common commands:

Make Calls:

• Say, "Hey Google, call [contact name]" to dial someone.

• Example: "Hey Google, call Mom."

Send Text Messages:

• Say, "Hey Google, send a text to [contact name]", then dictate your message.

• Example: "Hey Google, send a text to John saying 'I'll be there in 10 minutes.'"

Control Music and Media:

• Say, "Hey Google, play some music" or "Hey Google, play [song/artist]".

• In addition, you can pause, skip songs, adjust volume, and more.

Set Alarms and Reminders:

• Say, "Hey Google, remind me to go grocery shopping at 3 PM."

"Hey Google, set an alarm for 7 AM," for instance.

Obtain Directions:

• In Google Maps, type "Hey Google, navigate to [destination]" to obtain directions.

Google Assistant Integration with Other Apps

To make your phone smarter, Google Assistant integrates with a variety of third-party apps. Apps for music services, smart home appliances, and other things can be integrated.

Linking Smart Home Appliances:

1.Launch the Google Home application.

2.To add a device, tap the + symbol.

3.Connect your thermostat, smart lights, and other compatible devices by following the directions.

4.Once connected, you can control them with commands like these using Google Assistant:

o "Switch off the lights, Google."

o **"Set the temperature to 72 degrees, Google."**

Integration of Apps from Third Parties:
Apps like WhatsApp, YouTube, and Spotify can all be integrated with Google Assistant.

To link applications:

1.Go to Settings > Google > Search, Assistant & Voice > Google Assistant to access the Google Assistant settings.

2.Choose the app you wish to connect by scrolling to Services.

3.To connect the app to Google Assistant, follow the instructions.

Establishing Routines for Daily Tasks

By establishing routines, Google Assistant enables you to automate numerous tasks with a single command. This is excellent for routine tasks like setting alarms and shutting off lights, as well as receiving weather updates as soon as you wake up.

Establishing a Routine:

1."Hey Google" will launch Google Assistant.

2.Select Routines by tapping on the Profile icon.

3.Tap the + button to create a new routine.

4.Add actions such as:

o Turn on/off lights

o Read the news

o Play music

o Set a reminder

o Get the weather

5.Customize the routine by selecting a certain time or phrase to trigger it (e.g., "Good morning" to start your daily routine).

6.Save your routine.

Example of a Morning Routine:

• When you say, "Hey Google, good morning," Google Assistant could:

o Turn on the lights.

o Tell you the weather.

o Play your favorite playlist.

o Read your calendar events for the day.

Using Google Assistant for Hands-Free Navigation

Google Assistant is perfect for navigating when you're driving or walking and need to keep your hands free. Here's how to use it for hands-free navigation:

Getting Directions:

• Simply say, "Hey Google, navigate to [destination]".

• Google Assistant will open Google Maps and start giving you turn-by-turn directions.

Control Navigation During the Trip:

• You can also use voice commands during your trip:

o "Hey Google, what's my ETA?" to check the estimated time of arrival.

o "Hey Google, reroute" to find an alternate route.

o "Hey Google, stop navigation" to stop the directions.

Chapter 8: Configuring and Utilizing Applications

This chapter will cover managing app permissions and subscriptions, as well as how to download, manage, and arrange apps on your Google Pixel 9a.

Using the Google Play Store to download apps

You may download thousands of apps, games, and media to your Pixel 9a from the Google Play Store. To download an app, follow these steps:

Procedure for App Downloading:

1.Tap the Play Store icon to launch the Google Play Store.

2.Enter the name of the app you wish to download in the search box located at the top.

3.From the search results, pick the app.

4.To begin the app's download, tap the Install button.

5.You can tap Open to start the app when it has been installed.

Tip: You can install apps straight from the Google Play website on numerous devices connected to your Google account.

Handling Installed Applications

Apps are simple to handle once you've downloaded them. Here's how:

Examining Installed Applications:

1.Swiping up on the home screen will open the App Drawer.

2.To locate a particular app, use the search bar at the top or scroll through the list of apps.

App Updates:

1.Launch the Google Play Store.

2.To access My apps & games, tap the Menu symbol (three horizontal lines) in the upper-left corner.

3.A list of apps that require updates will appear. To update all apps, tap Update All. Alternatively, you may choose which apps to update.

Verifying App Information:

1.Navigate to My apps & games on the Play Store.

2.To get further information about an app, like its size, permissions, and version, tap on it.

Making Use of Google Play Subscriptions and Services

Music, movies, and cloud storage are among the services and subscriptions that Google Play provides. How to use them is as follows:

Taking Care of Subscriptions:

1.Launch the Google Play Store.

2.Choose Subscriptions after tapping the Menu icon.

3.Google Play Music, YouTube Premium, and other active subscriptions may be viewed and managed here.

Services for Google Play:

In addition to helping to handle features like authentication and synchronisation with Google services, Google Play Services operates in the background to keep your apps updated.

Tip: To guarantee that apps function correctly, make sure Google Play Services is up to date.

Sorting Applications into Folders

Keeping your home screen neat and making apps easy to access can be achieved by grouping them into folders.

How to Make an App Folder:

1.Hold down a tap on an app icon.

2.You can drag it over another app in the same folder.

3.You can press the folder name to change its name once it has been created.

Including Additional Apps in a Folder:

• Just drag more programs into the folder that already exists.

Controlling Permissions for Apps

You can manage which data, such as your location, camera, or contacts, apps may access on your Pixel 9a. To manage app permissions, follow these steps:

Permissions Granting and Revocation:

1.Navigate to [App Name] under Settings > Apps.

2.To check what the app may access, tap Permissions.

3.Activate or deactivate permissions as necessary.

Advice for privacy: Give apps only the rights required to perform their functions.

Removing Applications

You can quickly remove an app to make room if you no longer need it:

How to Remove an App:

1.Launch the App Drawer.

2.To uninstall an app, tap and hold it.

3.Choose Uninstall from the menu.

4.Tap OK to confirm.

Chapter 9: Battery Life Management

This chapter will cover how to monitor the health of your Pixel 9a's battery, manage its life, and utilize options that help it last longer.

Verifying the Health and Status of Batteries

To keep an eye on your Pixel 9a's health and battery life:

1.Navigate to Settings > Battery.

2.Here, you can view the battery's daily usage as well as details about its condition, such as charging cycles and lifespan.

Settings & Modes for Power Saving

When your battery is low on charge, power-saving capabilities might help it last longer.

Power Saver Enabled:

1.Navigate to Battery Saver under Settings > Battery.

2.To increase battery life and reduce background operations, turn on Battery Saver.

How to Increase Battery Life

1.Reduce Screen Brightness: Either manually reduce the brightness or use Adaptive Brightness.

2.Reduce Background Apps: Unused apps that drain battery in the background should be closed.

3.Turn off Unused Features: When not in use, turn off GPS, Bluetooth, and Wi-Fi.

4.Use Dark Mode: On OLED screens, Dark Mode can help save battery life.

Google Pixel 9a Charging (Wired and Wireless)

To get your Pixel 9a charged:

Charging via Wired:

1.Connect one end of the USB-C charging cable to a charger and the other end to your Pixel 9a.

2.Immediately, your phone will start charging.

Charging wirelessly:

• To charge your phone cordlessly, place it on a wireless charging pad if you have one.

Making Use of Battery Optimization Features

Limiting background programs is one way that battery optimization might lower battery consumption:

1.Navigate to Settings > Battery > Optimize Battery.

2.To restrict an app's background activities, tap Optimize next to it.

Knowing the Differences Between Adaptive and Fast Charging

Quick Charging:

• When plugged with a suitable charger, your Pixel 9a's fast charging feature charges your phone rapidly.

Adaptive Charging:

• Especially while charging overnight, adaptive charging maximizes the charging speed to safeguard the battery and increase its longevity.

You now have a comprehensive understanding of how to use apps, manage your battery, and make the most of Google Assistant on your Google Pixel 9a!

Chapter 10: Security and Data

Numerous features are included with your Google Pixel 9a to help you safeguard your data and device. We will go over the key security settings and recommended procedures in this chapter to protect your data.

Configuring a Secure Lock Screen (Password, Pattern, or PIN)

Setting up a lock screen with a PIN, pattern, or password is crucial for maintaining the security of your phone.

How to Configure a Lock Screen:

1.Select Screen Lock under Settings > Security.

2.Pick amongst the following options: password, PIN, or pattern.

3.Set up your preferred unlocking method for your phone by following the on-screen instructions.

Tip: We advise creating a strong password for optimal protection, particularly if your phone has private data.

Using Facial Recognition and Fingerprints for Security

You may unlock your Pixel 9a faster and more securely by using fingerprint and facial recognition in addition to conventional lock screens.

Configuring Unlocking Fingerprints:

1.Select Fingerprint under Settings > Security.

2.Put your finger on the sensor several times and follow the instructions to register your fingerprint.

3.Once configured, all you have to do is touch the fingerprint sensor on your phone to unlock it.

Configuring Face Unlock:

1.Navigate to Security > Settings > Face Unlock.

2.To have your face scanned for recognition, follow the instructions.

3.Once your phone is set up, all you have to do is look at it to unlock it.

Note: You can access your smartphone more quickly with both fingerprint and face unlock, but be aware that face unlock might not be as secure as a PIN, pattern, or password.

Configuring Google Find My Device

If your Pixel 9a is lost or stolen, Google's Find My Device can help you find it, lock it, or remove it.

How to Configure Find My Device:

1.Navigate to Find My Device under Settings > Security.

2.Verify that it is turned on. If you haven't already, you might need to log into your Google account.

3.You can find your phone on a map, remotely lock it, or remove all data if you misplace it by going to the Find My Device website (or using the app on a different device).

Controlling Privacy Settings and App Permissions

You can manage the data that apps can access on your Pixel 9a. This covers items like your camera, contacts, and location.

How to Control Permissions for Apps:

1.Navigate to Permission Manager under Settings > Privacy.

2.You can see and manage the information that each app may access, such as your microphone, location, and camera. To change an app's permissions, tap on it.

Advice: Choose which apps you provide authorization to use. Only grant access that is required for the application to operate.

Creating a backup and recovering your data

You can prevent the loss of crucial data, including contacts, images, and app data, by backing up your data.

How to Make a Data Backup:

1.Navigate to Settings > Backup > Google.

2.To automatically save data, including contacts, apps, call logs, images, and videos, turn on backup to Google Drive.

How to Get Your Data Back:

• You can restore your data from an earlier backup during the initial setup process when configuring a new Pixel device or following a factory reset. To restore your backed-up data, just log into your Google account.

Using Google Services with Two-Factor Authentication

Adding two-factor authentication (2FA) to your Google account increases its security. To log in, you need to provide your password and complete an additional verification step.

How to Make Two-Factor Authentication Active:

1.On your Pixel 9a, open Google Settings or the Google Play Store.

2.Select 2-Step Verification under Security.

3.To activate 2FA, follow the directions using a physical security key, Google Authenticator, or text message.

Having 2FA enabled will prevent someone from accessing your account without the second factor of authentication, even if they manage to figure out your password.

Chapter 11: Handling Files and Storage

To guarantee seamless operation and plenty of room for fresh information, it's critical to manage the storage and files on your device. Let's explore how to manage apps, transfer data, and check your storage.

Verifying Your Pixel 9a's Storage Capacity

To determine how much space is still available on your device:

1.Navigate to Settings > Storage.

2.An summary of your available storage space and the amount of storage that programs, pictures, movies, and other items are using can be found here.

Advice: You can use the Free up space feature to remove unnecessary files or apps from your storage if it's almost full.

Transferring Data Between the SD Card and Internal Storage (if appropriate)

You can clear up space by transferring files between the internal storage and the SD card if your Pixel 9a supports them.

How to Transfer Files:

1.Launch the Files application.

2.Choose the file (such as a document or photo) that you wish to transfer.

3.Choose Move to after tapping the three dots in the upper-right corner.

4.Move the file and select your SD card as the destination.

Using Cloud Storage with Google Drive

You may use Google Drive to back up crucial documents, images, and data, and it offers 15 GB of free cloud storage.

How to Add Documents to Google Drive:

1.Launch the Google Drive application.

2.To upload a file, tap the plus symbol.

3.Choose the file you wish to upload from your device by selecting Upload.

Using the Files App to Manage Files

You can manage, find, and arrange your files with the aid of the Files app.

The Files App's features include:

• Browse files: You may quickly see every file that is saved on your device.

• Search: Look for particular files quickly.

• Clean up: The software offers advice on how to get rid of extraneous files, like cached information or duplicate images.

Managing Space and Eliminating Files

You could choose to remove unnecessary files to free up storage.

How to Remove Files:

1.Launch the Files application.

2.Choose the file you want to remove.

3.To remove the file, tap the trash can icon.

4.You can also go to Settings > Storage > Cache data and clear the cached data to make room.

Using Google Photos to Store Pictures and Videos

Your images and videos are automatically backed up to the cloud via Google Photos, ensuring their safety and accessibility across all devices.

How to Make a Photo Backup:

1.Launch the Google Photos application.

2.Go to Settings > Backup & sync after tapping the Menu icon (three lines).

3.Turn on backup and sync to have your pictures and videos automatically backed up.

Chapter 12 Customizing Your Google Pixel 9a

You can make your Google Pixel 9a genuinely unique by personalizing it. You may alter almost every feature of your phone, from the wallpaper to the system settings.

Modifying the Themes and Wallpaper

The wallpaper on your lock screen, home screen, or both can be changed. Themes can also be used to create a distinctive appearance.

How to Change Your Wallpaper:

1.On the home screen, tap and hold.

2.Choose your style and wallpaper.

3. You can select themes that alter the appearance of your phone, your own images, or the default wallpapers.

Changing the Home Screen and Lock Screen Settings

Widgets, app icons, and shortcuts can be used to personalize the home screen and lock screen of your Pixel 9a.

In order to alter the home screen:

1. On the home screen, tap and hold.

2. To change the grid layout, app icons, and icon size, select Home settings.

3. To add widgets, select Widgets after holding down an empty area on the home screen.

Modifying the Animation Speed, Display, and System Font

For a more seamless experience, you can change the screen display, text size, and even animation speed.

How to Modify the Display:

1.Select Font size under Settings > Display.

2.Select the font size that works best for you.

3.Go to Developer settings (Settings > About phone, touch 7 times on Build number) and change the Animation scale.

Configuring Other Display Settings and Dark Mode

On OLED screens, dark mode prolongs battery life and lessens eye strain. It can be enabled in individual apps or throughout your system.

How to Turn on Dark Mode:

1.Navigate to Display > Settings > Dark theme.

2.Turn it on to activate a dark mode for the entire system.

Another option is to program dark mode to activate automatically at sunset or at a predetermined period.

Settings for Sound and Notifications

Changing the sound and notification settings on your phone allows you to customize system notifications, ringtones, and alerts for various apps.

Changing the Sound Configuration:

1.Select Sound under Settings.

2.From here, you may alter volume levels, select different ringtones for calls, notifications, and alarms, and manage Do Not Disturb settings.

Creating Custom Shortcuts for Apps

To make accessing apps quicker, you can build custom shortcuts on your home screen.

How to Establish a Shortcut:

1.In the app drawer, tap and hold an app.

2.Drag the application to the home screen or choose Add shortcut.

Chapter 13: Enhanced Functionalities

Some cutting-edge features on the Pixel 9a will help you make the most of your gadget. These features, which range from digital wellbeing to smart home control, will improve your experience.

Utilizing a Smart Home Configuration with the Google Pixel 9a

You can use Google Assistant on your Pixel 9a to control smart home appliances like lights, thermostats, and security cameras.

Putting Focus Mode and Digital Wellbeing in Place

By measuring screen time, establishing app limitations, and using Focus Mode to create distraction-free environments, Digital

Wellbeing assists you in managing your phone usage.

How to Put Yourself in Focus Mode:

1.Navigate to Settings > Parental controls & Digital Wellbeing.

2.Choose which apps to turn off while you need to concentrate by tapping on Focus Mode.

Controlling App Limits and Screen Time

Manage your device use by keeping track of your screen time and establishing limitations for particular apps.

Configuring and Tailoring Gesture Navigation

You can slide and navigate without using buttons thanks to the Pixel 9a's gesture navigation capability.

Using Visual Search with Google Lens

You may use Google Lens to look for text or objects by aiming your camera at them.

Exploring the Pixel 9a's "Now Playing" Feature

Songs that are playing around you are automatically identified by the Now Playing feature.

Chapter 13 ends there. To get the most out of your Pixel 9a, keep reading the rest of the guide!

Chapter 14: Interaction with Other Electronic Devices

Whether you want to use your Google Pixel 9a as a personal hotspot, share files, or connect to smart home systems, it's built to connect with other devices with ease. The several methods for connecting and integrating your Pixel 9a with other devices are covered in this chapter.

Using Chromecast to Connect the Pixel 9a to a TV or Projector

Casting material from your Pixel 9a to a compatible TV or projector is possible using Chromecast. This is ideal for displaying presentations, sharing pictures, and watching films.

How to Utilize Chromecast:

1.Make sure the Chromecast device is configured correctly before connecting your TV or projector.

2.Tap Cast after swiping down the Quick Settings menu on your Pixel 9a.

3.From the list of options, pick your Chromecast-capable device.

4.After connecting, you can begin casting videos from Google Photos, YouTube, and Netflix, among other apps.

Make sure your Chromecast and Pixel 9a are linked to the same wireless network.

Creating a Hotspot with the Google Pixel 9a

You can use your Pixel 9a as a mobile hotspot to share your phone's internet connection with other devices, such as a laptop or tablet.

Steps to Set Up a Mobile Hotspot:

1.Go to Settings > Network & internet > Hotspot & tethering.

2.Toggle the Wi-Fi hotspot on by tapping on it.

3.By selecting Hotspot settings, you can change your hotspot's parameters, including the network name and password.

4.Once configured, other devices can use the Wi-Fi network name and password to connect to the hotspot.

Advice: If you use mobile data, pay attention to how much you use because it may quickly mount up when you have several devices connected.

Configuring External Device Connection via USB OTG

With a USB cord and an OTG adapter, you can utilize USB OTG (On-The-Go) to connect external devices to your Pixel 9a, such as a game controller, USB drive, keyboard, or mouse.

How to Utilize USB OTG:

1.Connect the OTG adapter to your Pixel 9a's USB-C connector.

2.Attach the external device (such as a USB keyboard or disc) to the OTG adapter's opposite end.

3.You should be able to utilize or transmit data from your Pixel 9a as soon as it recognizes the device.

Advice: In order for certain external devices to function with your Pixel 9a, you may need to install extra apps or software.

Connecting Wearables (Google Fit, Wear OS Devices) to the Pixel 9a

To keep you connected and monitor your health, your Pixel 9a can sync with a variety of wearable technology, including fitness trackers and smartwatches.

How to Connect Wear OS Devices:

1.On your Pixel 9a, launch the Wear OS by Google app.

2.To sync your Pixel 9a with your Wear OS device—such as a Google Pixel Watch or other Wear OS smartwatches—follow the on-screen instructions.

3.Make sure Bluetooth is turned on during the pairing process, then follow the directions to finish connecting.

Advice: When pairing your wearable with your Pixel 9a, make sure it is both charged and within Bluetooth range.

Using Nearby Share to Share Files

Sending files, links, and images between Android devices in close proximity without requiring an internet connection is quick and simple with Nearby Share.

How to Use Nearby Share to Share Files:

1.Open the document or photo that you wish to share.

2.From the list of sharing choices, choose Nearby Share after tapping the Share icon.

3.The Pixel 9a will look for devices in the vicinity. Decide which gadget you wish to share.

4.A prompt to accept the file transfer will be sent to the other device. The file will be emailed after it is approved.

Advice: Make sure both devices are within Bluetooth range of one another and that Nearby Share is turned on.

How to Use Android Auto in Your Vehicle

To access apps, navigation, and communication capabilities while driving, you may link your Pixel 9a to your car's infotainment system using Android Auto.

How to Configure Android Auto:

1.Verify that the system in your vehicle is USB or Bluetooth linked and that Android Auto is supported.

2.If it isn't already installed, download and install the Android Auto app from the Google Play Store.

3.Use a USB cord to connect your Pixel 9a to your vehicle (or wirelessly, if compatible).

4.To grant Android Auto the required permissions, including location and contacts, adhere to the instructions.

5.Once linked, you may use the infotainment screen in your car to play music, make calls, use Google Maps, and more.

Advice: Android Auto was created to make using it while driving safer. To reduce distractions and control features, use voice

Chapter 15: FAQs and Troubleshooting

The usual problems you could run into with your Google Pixel 9a are fixed in this chapter. Before getting more assistance, try the following troubleshooting actions if you're having issues.

Typical Problems and Solutions (App crashes, Wi-Fi issues, etc.)

Wi-Fi Issues:

• Issue: Wi-Fi keeps disconnecting or won't connect.

o Fix: Restart both your Pixel 9a and your router. Reconnect after forgetting the Wi-Fi network in Settings > Network & internet > Wi-Fi if the problem continues.

App Failures:

• Issue: Applications frequently freeze or crash.

o Fix: Try using Settings > Apps to force-stop the application. Reinstall the app after uninstalling it if the problem persists.

How to Handle a Freezing or Unresponsive Pixel 9a

Try the following if your Pixel 9a freezes or stops responding:

How to Perform a Force Restart:

1.For roughly ten seconds, press and hold the Power and Volume Down buttons at the same time.

2.After your phone restarts, any small problems that were causing the freezing should be fixed.

As a final resort, try doing a factory reset (discussed in the following section) if this doesn't work.

Restoring the Factory Settings on Your Google Pixel 9a

A factory reset can return your phone to its original condition if you're having ongoing problems or intend to sell or give it away.

How to Complete a Factory Reset:

1.Navigate to System > Settings > Reset options.

2.Erase all data (factory reset) is tapped.

3.To remove all data from your device, confirm the action and adhere to the instructions.

Warning: Before performing a factory reset, be sure to backup your data because it will erase all of your personal information from the phone.

Handling Low Storage Problems
Answer:

• Get rid of apps or files that aren't needed.

• Transfer files to an SD card (if compatible) or Google Drive.

• To manage and delete cache data, use the Files app.

How to Handle a Non-Charging Phone
Answer:

• Verify that the adapter and charging cord are operating correctly. Try a different charger or cord.

• Check for dust or dirt in the charging port. If necessary, gently clean it.

• Try charging again after doing a soft reset, which involves holding down the power button for ten seconds.

Reaching out to Google Support

Contact Google Support if the problems continue or if you require help with more complex troubleshooting.

How to Get in Touch with Google Help:

1.Navigate to Settings > Feedback & Help.

2.To reach the support page and speak with a Google professional, tap Contact us.

Chapter 16: Updating and Maintaining Software

Maintaining the most recent software on your Pixel 9a guarantees that it is safe and operating effectively. We will walk you through the update procedure and provide general maintenance advice in this chapter.

How to Look for Updates in Software

Check for software updates on a frequent basis to make sure your phone is running the most recent version of Android and security patches.

Procedure for Looking for Updates:

1.Navigate to Settings > System > Update software.

2.Updates will be checked on your phone. Tap Download to install any updates that are available.

Advice: While downloading updates, keep your Pixel 9a charged and connected to Wi-Fi.

Installing Security Patches and System Updates

System updates include vital security patches that shield your device from vulnerabilities in addition to enhancing performance.

Procedure for Installing Updates:

1.When an update becomes available, select "Download" and proceed to install it.

2.To install the update, adhere to the instructions. During the procedure, your phone might restart.

Comprehending the Update Schedule for the Pixel 9a

Google releases at least one significant Android upgrade year and security patches for the Pixel 9a on a monthly basis.

For additional information on when updates are available for your device, consult Google's official update schedule.

Optimizing System Performance and Clearing the Cache

Clear the system cache and unnecessary programs on a regular basis to ensure seamless operation.

How to Empty the Cache:

1.Navigate to Settings > Storage.

2. Tap Cache data and select Clear to clear temporary files.

Tip: Clearing cache won't remove personal data, but it may speed up certain programs.

Factory Reset Instructions and When to Do It

A factory reset can be performed if you're facing issues that can't be fixed by ordinary troubleshooting, or when you're planning to sell your device.

Keeping Apps Up to Date

Ensure your apps are up to date to benefit from new features and bug fixes.

Steps to Update Apps:

1. Launch the Google Play Store.

2. Tap the Menu icon (three lines) > My applications & games.

3.To update the installed apps, tap Update all.

Using Google Services in Chapter 17

To improve your Pixel 9a experience, Google offers a number of services. You will learn how to utilize Google Maps, sync your accounts, and access other services like Google Pay in this chapter.

Syncing Gmail, Calendar, and Contacts on Google

For smooth device integration, your Pixel 9a syncs Google Calendar, Contacts, and Gmail automatically.

How to Sync:

1.Navigate to Settings > Sync > Google.

2.Turn on Gmail, Calendar, and Contacts to sync your data between devices.

Using Google Maps to Share Locations and Navigate

Your go-to app for navigation and sharing your whereabouts with loved ones is Google Maps.

How to Utilize Google Maps:

1.Launch the Google Maps application.

2.To begin navigation, enter your destination and select Directions.

3.The program also allows you to share your current location with other users.

Getting into Google Docs and Drive

Your cloud storage for files, documents, and images is Google Drive. You can create, edit, and share documents online with Google Docs.

How to Utilize Google Drive:

1.To access your files, launch the Google Drive application.

2.To upload files or use Google Docs to create new documents, tap +.

Managing Payment Methods and Configuring Google Pay

You can use your phone to safely make payments using Google Pay. Tickets and loyalty cards can also be stored.

How to Configure Google Pay:

1.Open the Google Pay app after downloading it.

2.As directed by the on-screen instructions, add a payment method.

Using the Google Home App to Control Your Smart Home

All of your smart home devices can be managed and controlled from a single location with the Google Home app.

How to Utilize Google Home:

1.Launch the Google Home application.

2.To configure and manage your smart devices, adhere to the instructions.

Investigating Google Stadia for Video Games

With Google Stadia, you can play games straight from your Pixel 9a without having to download them.

How to Use Stadia on Google:

1.Go to the Google Play Store and download the Stadia app.

2.Choose a game from the selection, then begin playing it straight from the cloud.

That concludes this extensive guide. Now you're ready to make the most of your Pixel 9a!